⚛ Smithsonian

PREHISTORIC

WRITTEN BY
KATHLEEN WEIDNER ZOEHFELD

ILLUSTRATIONS BY
JULIUS CSOTONYI

What on Earth Books

What on Earth Books is an imprint of What on Earth Publishing
The Black Barn, Wickhurst Farm, Tonbridge, Kent TN11 8PS, United Kingdom
30 Ridge Road, Unit B, Greenbelt, Maryland 20770, United States

First published in the United States in 2019

Written by Kathleen Weidner Zoehfeld
Text copyright © 2019 What on Earth Publishing Ltd

Produced in association with Smithsonian's National Museum of Natural History:
Sant Director of the National Museum of Natural History Director: Kirk R. Johnson
David H. Koch Hall of Fossils content team: Anna K. Behrensmeyer, Kara Blond, Amy Bolton,
Matthew T. Carrano, Laura Donnelly-Smith, Elizabeth Jones, Michael Lawrence, Matthew T. Miller,
Juliana Olsson, Meg Rivers, Angela Roberts Reeder, Siobhan Starrs, Scott L. Wing

The name of the Smithsonian Institution and the sunburst are registered trademarks of the Smithsonian Institution

All illustrations, unless otherwise credited, are by Julius Csotonyi
Pages 8–9, 10, 12–13, 15, 16, 20, 27, 29, 24–25, 32–33, 36–37, 38 © Smithsonian Institution
Pages 30 © Julius Csotonyi and the Houston Museum of Natural Science
Pages 19, 22, 42 © Julius Csotonyi
Cover illustration © Julius Csotonyi

Additional illustrations and photography:
Pages 3, 5, 7, 9, 11, 14, 15, 18, 21, 23, 25, 26, 27, 31, 32, 35, 37, 40, 45 by Andrey Atuchin © Smithsonian Institution
Pages 34, 41 by John Gurche © Smithsonian Institution
Page 6 iStock.com/Sean Pavone

Staff for this book:
Patrick Skipworth, editor
Assunção Sampayo, designer
Andy Forshaw, cover design

Library of Congress Cataloging-in-Publication Data available upon request

ISBN: 978-1-912920-05-1

Printed in China

10 9 8 7 6 5 4 3 2 1

whatonearthbooks.com

CONTENTS

INTRODUCTION

ANTHROPOCENE

PRESENT DAY

Humans live everywhere on planet Earth. We live close to the sea and on high mountain slopes. We live on wide-open plains and in dense forests. Some of us live in houses in the country, and others in apartment buildings in big cities.

We travel to work and to our schools in cars and buses. We shop for clothes, toys, and other goods that are made in factories all around the world. The food we eat is grown on farms and brought to us by boat, train, or truck. If our friends are far away, we talk to them using smartphones and computers. And if we want to explore an exciting new place, we hop on a plane and fly there.

This is our everyday world.

This is Earth today.

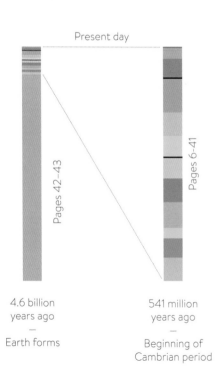

We share our planet with millions of other species. Sometimes, humans are able to exist in harmony with these species. But often our way of life can have a negative impact on other living things. The white rhinoceros is one animal threatened with extinction. Humans have destroyed much of its natural habitat and hunted it for its meat and horns.

ABOUT THE PREHISTORIC TIMELINE

In this book you will travel backwards in time billions of years. Right now you're in the present day—the Anthropocene Epoch. Turn the page to start traveling back through time!

If you ever get lost on your journey, take a look at the timeline bar on the right edge of the page to find out where you are. The trip is so long, that for most of this book (pages 6–41) this timeline can only show from the present day to around 541 million years ago, the beginning of the Cambrian Period. But the real history of the Earth is much longer—around 4.6 billion years. You can see what a whole timeline of the Earth's history looks like on pages 42–43.

Present day

Pages 42–43

Pages 6–41

4.6 billion
years ago
—
Earth forms

541 million
years ago
—
Beginning of
Cambrian period

HOLOCENE

10,000 YEARS AGO–PRESENT DAY

Humans evolved during an ice age. For most of this time, life was tough. Temperatures were low. The polar ice caps were more than just caps—they were more like ice cloaks. But around ten thousand years ago, Earth entered a warming spell scientists call the Holocene, and the ice sheets began to shrink.

This was good for humans. Before long, people were living all around the globe, wandering across prairies, through forests, and along coastlines in small groups. They hunted and fished for food or gathered roots, nuts, and fruits to eat while they traveled.

As the climate continued to warm, some groups settled in small villages and began to farm the land. They chose places where the soil was good for growing crops and with plenty of fresh water nearby in rivers or lakes. Over time, some of those villages grew into the first towns and cities. Today, most people live in urban areas.

Even with this warming, we are actually still living in an ice age today. It may not feel like it on a hot summer day, but as long as there's at least some ice and snow at the North and South Poles, scientists say it's an ice age.

Earth today, during ice age conditions

Earth during the warm Cretaceous Period 70 million years ago

Large mammals such as woolly mammoths, mastodons, and woolly rhinos still roamed the Earth at the beginning of the Holocene. But within a couple of thousand years, they were all extinct. Along with the changing climate, humans hunting with early weapons may have been partially responsible for their disappearance.

ICE AGES

"The Ice Age" during which we evolved began 2.6 million years ago. Since then, the Earth has alternated between times of warming and cooling. But throughout this time, the Earth's poles have always been covered by ice sheets.

There have been four other ice ages before the current one. Around 650 million years ago, the Earth may have been so cold that it was totally frozen over. Ice sheets stretched all the way to the Equator. This period is called "Snowball Earth."

"Snowball Earth," 650 million years ago

PLEISTOCENE

2.6 MILLION–10,000 YEARS AGO

The time we call "the Ice Age" began 2.6 million years ago at the start of the Pleistocene Epoch. During this time, Earth's climate cooled. Ice caps formed at the North and South Poles, and the planet began diving into a long, deep cold spell. At times, thick fingers of ice reached nearly a third of the way down to the Equator.

But the long history of the Ice Age has been punctuated by several warmer times too, when glaciers and ice sheets retreated. Scientists call the cold times "glacial periods" and the warmer ones "interglacials."

During the warmer interglacial periods, the environment provided plenty of water from melting glaciers. Forests flourished and mammals—at least some of them—grew to extraordinary sizes! Giant ground sloths stripped leaves from trees and huge armored glyptodonts skulked across forests and plains. Saber-toothed cats stalked their prey through the long grass.

When cold conditions returned in full force, many types of large mammals went extinct. The animals that survived the change were the ones best adapted for the cold weather—like the huge woolly mammoths and musk oxen, with their thick fur coats.

CLIMATE CHANGE

Changing temperatures had drastic effects on life on Earth during the Pleistocene Epoch. But why does the climate change over time?

Scientists have found clues in rock layers and fossils. They also look closely at ice cores taken from deep within ancient glaciers and ice sheets, which are formed from snow compressed over hundreds of thousands of years. The recent cold and warm cycles of Earth's climate are thought to have been caused, in part, by changes in Earth's orbit around the Sun and in the way Earth wobbles, like a top, as it spins.

Today, the climate is warming up once again. But scientists have pointed to a different cause. Humans are affecting the climate, especially from burning fossil fuels such as coal and natural gas. These fuels add greenhouse gases to the atmosphere. As the amount of greenhouse gases goes up, more and more heat from the Sun gets trapped, and the Earth gets warmer.

The 8-inch- (30cm-) long canine teeth of the saber-toothed cat *Smilodon* were used for stabbing and tearing into its prey. Its enormous size meant *Smilodon* needed to be able to flex its jaw 90 degrees to take a full bite.

Some heat escapes from the Earth's atmosphere into space

Some heat is trapped in the atmosphere by greenhouse gases and warms the Earth

Sun's rays

Earth's atmosphere, including greenhouse gases

NEOGENE

23 MILLION–2.6 MILLION YEARS AGO

From hot humid rain forests to cool, windswept grasslands, mammals first began to dominate the Earth's ecosystems during the Neogene Period. Some types developed large bodies. Others could run long distances or swim in the ocean. Birds, reptiles, amphibians, and insects diversified into new forms too. These adaptations allowed them to thrive in the new ecosystems.

On the land, giant plant-eaters munched on soft grasses and herbs. Elephant-sized *Gomphotherium* used its lower tusks to dig juicy roots out of the mud. The largest of them weighed over 6.5 tons.

Other smaller mammals lived mostly underground. *Ceratogaulus* is sometimes called the "horned gopher." It used its horns to dig burrows. Many types of mammals have horns, but *Ceratogaulus* is the only known rodent that ever did!

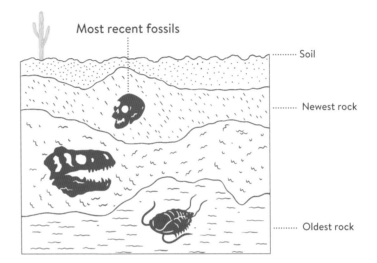

In the oceans of the Neogene Period, marine mammals such as dolphins, whales, and seals (including *Acrophoca*, shown top left chasing a banded penguin) were some of the top predators. But at the top of the food chain were giant sharks such as *Megalodon* (seen here lurking in the background).

FANTASTIC FOSSILS

Fossils are the remains of animals, plants, and other living things, preserved over millions of years. Paleontologists study fossils to learn about living things from long ago.

Most fossils are formed when a living thing dies and gets buried in a layer of sand or mud that turns into rock and preserves it. Rock layers that form during a particular period contain only fossils from that period. So if you're planning to dig up dinosaurs, you'd want to look in an older rock layer than if you were searching for giant mammals.

Most recent fossils

Soil

Newest rock

Oldest rock

PALEOGENE

66 MILLION–23 MILLION YEARS AGO

Lush forests covered the Earth during the Paleogene Period. Our planet's climate was warm, and new types of mammals were appearing. The world's first flying mammals—the bats—took to the air. They flew among the branches to feed on fruits and insects.

The world's first primates took to the trees then too. We humans are primates. These early types are our distant relatives.

Small mammals may have felt a bit intimidated by the giant *Diatryma*. This 7-foot- (2.1m-) tall flightless bird was a distant relative of our own chickens and turkeys. Fortunately, its huge beak was for crushing seeds, not prey.

Sun

Sky

Tree

Bird

Fox

Rock

Lake

ECOSYSTEMS

Thick rain forests grew up in the warm Paleogene climate. New types of living things developed in these lush environments, feasting on fruits and berries.

Scientists call the place where a species lives its "ecosystem." An ecosystem can be a fast-flowing river, a grassy savannah, or even the branches of a single tree. In desert or polar ecosystems, life can be restricted to only a handful of different plants and animals. But rain forest ecosystems contain a great diversity of species. Scientists have recorded over 400,000 species in the Amazon rain forest alone. It is estimated that over 1 million more species have yet to be discovered in the Amazon ecosystem.

Notharctus was one of the first primate ancestors. It used its grasping hands to climb high in the trees and reach for delicious fruits.

Diatryma's wings were small and not suited for flying. But it could probably run really fast, like an ostrich today.

END-CRETACEOUS

EXTINCTION

66 MILLION YEARS AGO

A single event can drastically change the course of life on Earth. One terrible day 66 million years ago an asteroid the size of Mount Everest struck the Earth. It was a day just like any other for the animals that lived then. Plant-eaters munched on their favorite fruits. Big predators pounced on tasty little mammals and lizards. Then, suddenly, everything went wrong.

A giant fireball glowed overhead, as bright as a second Sun. It sped through the air at about 67,000 miles per hour (108,000 km/h) and crashed near what is now the town of Chicxulub, in Mexico. The whole Earth shook like a gong. Molten rock and dust shot high into the sky. Fireballs rained down everywhere, and forests burned for thousands of miles around. Thick smoke and dust spread across the globe, blotting out the sunlight.

Without sunlight, plants died. Large plant-eating animals died too without their food. The meat-eaters fed desperately on the dead, until there was nothing left. One group in particular were wiped out almost entirely—the dinosaurs!

MASS EXTINCTIONS

During Earth's long history, cataclysmic events have brought life close to being totally eradicated. Scientists call these periods "mass extinctions." Five have taken place so far.

Scientists think that right now humans are causing a 6th mass extinction. Pollution, habitat destruction, and rapid global warming due to our burning of fossil fuels are threatening many species. But this also means we have the power to stop this mass extinction

THE BIG FIVE EXTINCTIONS

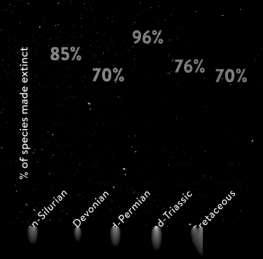

% of species made extinct

85% 96% 70% 76% 70%

n-Silurian Devonian d-Permian d-Triassic Cretaceous

CRETACEOUS

145–66 MILLION YEARS AGO

Dinosaurs of all shapes and sizes thrived in every environment on land during the Cretaceous Period. Tyrannosaurs, such as *Gorgosaurus*, were enormous meat-eating dinosaurs that roamed floodplains and forests, looking for meals. But plant-eating dinosaurs were developing some amazing defenses against them too. *Spinops* had a thick, bony frill around its neck that worked like a shield, to ward off tyrannosaur bites. Sharp horns on its face also helped the *Spinops* protect itself and its babies.

The duck-billed dinosaur *Edmontosaurus* had another strategy for staying safe. They did what many plant-eaters, such as zebras or buffalo, still do today—they lived in large herds. In a herd, there are many eyes to spot enemies and to call out early warnings. At the first sign of danger, the herd would all run at once. A herd's sudden movements confuse predators, giving the prey a better chance of escape.

Plants can't run away from the animals that eat them. But they do have other defenses. During the Cretaceous, a new kind of plant appeared that could take in more moisture and grow and recover much faster than the conifers and ferns that had dominated for millions of years. These were the angiosperms, or flowering plants.

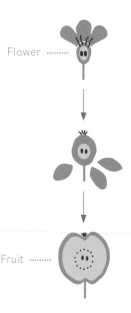

Flower ....

Fruit ....

The short crest on *Edmontosaurus*'s head may have been for attracting a mate. In some related species, these crests are made of hollow bone. Scientists think these dinosaurs might have used them to make sounds, like blowing into a trumpet.

FLOWERING PLANTS

Today flowers, which first developed during the Cretaceous, are not only a source of color and beauty—they are essential for our daily lives. All of our fruits and vegetables, as well as most of our grains, such as oats and wheat, come from flowering plants. We use wood from flowering trees to build homes, furniture, and many other things.

Marine reptiles came in many shapes and sizes too during the Cretaceous—from the ferocious mosasaur, *Tylosaurus*, to huge sea turtles such as *Protostega*. Ammonites and other marine invertebrates had thick shells or sharp spines to help protect them from being eaten.

OIL AND GAS

Most of the oil and gasoline that make our cars run formed in the Cretaceous seas. Tiny animals and plants called plankton lived in the sunlit waters. As they died, they settled to the bottom. Over the course of millions of years, layer upon layer built up. Intense heat and pressure underground changed some of the layers into the oil and gas we drill for today, millions of years later.

Oil that began to form in the Cretaceous is used today as fuel. But burning these polluting products in such great quantities is also causing environmental problems around the globe.

Up in the air were pterosaurs, leathery-winged reptiles distantly related to dinosaurs. Many toothless species of pterosaur flew over inland seas, in search of fish and other prey.

OVER **1 MILLION PLASTIC BOTTLES** ARE BOUGHT GLOBALLY EVERY MINUTE

Some plastic materials are made from oil that formed in the Cretaceous Period. While plastic is useful, it takes thousands of years to decompose. Lots ends up as pollution in oceans and rivers. Recycling it can help to reduce this problem.

Some tyrannosaur fossils, such as from this *Yutyrannus*, have been found with feathers. These were probably for keeping warm and showing off to mates, not for flight.

JURASSIC

201–145 MILLION YEARS AGO

Archaeopteryx was a feathered dinosaur that could fly. It had many things in common with modern birds. In fact, scientists think that birds are a special type of dinosaur—dinosaurs really have survived until the present day!

During the Jurassic, the world's largest land-living animals appeared. These were the biggest species of the four-legged, long-necked sauropods, which had first developed in the Triassic period. All over the world, the climate was warm, and the land was covered in ferns and horsetails or shaded by tall conifers and ginkgoes. Herds of sauropods trampled the vegetation and stripped the trees and bushes as they moved along.

Like birds—our own living dinosaurs—all types of dinosaurs laid eggs. But no matter how big a dinosaur got, its eggs could be no larger than a football. Any bigger, and the shell would have to be so thick, the baby inside wouldn't be able to get enough air. So, all dinosaurs were born small—even giant sauropods. Many dinosaur parents kept a close watch for any predators that might want to snatch one of their hatchlings. But to be truly safe, dinosaurs had to grow quickly. In less than 20 years, most reached full size, whether they grew to the size of a chicken or a bus.

Before the Jurassic Period, most of Earth's continents were connected in one giant supercontinent called Pangea. But during the Jurassic Period, the continents began to break up into the ones we know today. North America separated from Europe and Asia, forming the Atlantic Ocean. Late in the Jurassic, Africa began to split from South America too.

CHANGING CONTINENTS

Earth is made up of layers. On the top is a hard, brittle layer of rock called the lithosphere. Under that is a deep layer of very hot, squishy rock called the mantle. The lithosphere is broken up into several huge, continent-sized pieces called plates. These plates move very slowly—at about the speed our fingernails grow—as the hot, slowly flowing layer, the mantle, pushes and pulls them from below.

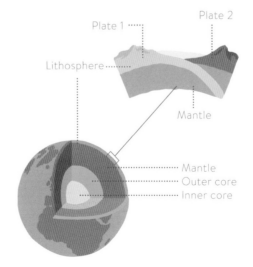

Plate 1

Plate 2

Lithosphere

Mantle

Mantle
Outer core
Inner core

TRIASSIC

252–201 MILLION YEARS AGO

Many new and amazing species populated the land during the Triassic Period. The world's first turtles, lizards, frogs, and mammals lived at this time. But the largest-bodied animals of all were from a group called the archosaurs. These reptiles included the ancestors of crocodiles, pterosaurs, and dinosaurs.

Herrerasaurus, one of the first dinosaurs, lived around 230 million years ago. In many areas of the supercontinent, forests of conifers and cycads, and meadows of ferns and horsetails provided good habitats for dinosaurs. Soon they had spread across the globe. Most of them were sharp-toothed predators that could run fast on two legs.

But during the Triassic, dinosaurs weren't in control yet. Most were small and meek compared to their huge crocodile-like cousins, such as *Smilosuchus*. These giants could take down big prey. If a hungry dinosaur wanted to grab a bite, it would have to tiptoe around the crocs!

WALK LIKE A DINOSAUR

Lizards and salamanders walk with their legs sprawled out to the sides, but all dinosaurs walk upright, with their legs underneath their bodies. Dinosaurs' feet have three main toes and hinge-like ankles that can move back and forth but not side to side.

The earliest dinosaurs had strong arms, with grasping hands. They walked on two legs and ate meat. Later groups included dinosaurs of many sizes, postures, and diets. But the basic structure of their legs stayed the same.

New animal groups found success during the Triassic Period, including the first dinosaurs. *Herrerasaurus* was a frightening meat-eating dinosaur that could reach 20 feet (6 m) long. Even so, it was dwarfed by the giant crocodile-like archosaurs of the time.

Dinosaur leg structure

Reptile leg structure (lizard)

As the first dinosaurs were spreading across the land, some reptiles returned to the sea. Unlike fish, marine reptiles need to come up to the surface to breathe air. Some, such as the needle-toothed *Askeptosaurus* (main image, top right), fed on fishes. Others, like *Paraplacodus* (main image, left), had broad, flat teeth for crushing hard-shelled invertebrates such as ammonites.

Alongside these marine reptiles, sharks and other types of fish were taking on new streamlined forms too. The earliest examples of most of the types of fishes we know (and eat!) today lived during the Triassic.

Ichthyosaurs were meat-eating marine animals that look a bit like dolphins. But these deadly predators were reptiles, not mammals.

MAMMALS

Among the new animals that emerged during the Triassic Period were the world's first true mammals. Their complex teeth allowed them a wide variety of ways to nip, slice, dice, and chew lots of types of food, including plants, insects, and eggs.

These early mammals still laid shelled eggs, just as their earlier, more reptile-like ancestors did. But today, all mammals except for the platypus and echidna give birth to live young.

MAMMALS TODAY FIT INTO THREE GROUPS

Most mammals, including humans, are placentals. They give birth to live young.

Marsupials give birth to live young, but they are not very developed. After being born, they continue their growth in a pouch.

Monotremes lay eggs. They are the smallest group.

Adelobasileus was a close relative of the first mammals. Like it, they were mostly small and lived similar lives to many rodents today.

END-PERMIAN

252 MILLION YEARS AGO

Are you prepared to travel back to a truly terrible time—252 million years ago—to witness the worst catastrophe in the history of the Earth? The trouble began in the area we now call Siberia, in Russia. Deep underground, red-hot rock was slowly rising, melting, and collecting to form a huge underground pool of magma called a hotspot.

Eventually, the pressure from the hotspot below became too great for the Earth's crust to take. Long cracks opened up and, for more than a million years, lava flows poured out in pulses. Over time, lava seared a vast area of land—roughly the size of the western United States. Dust, soot, and deadly gases from these volcanic eruptions filled the air. Huge amounts of the greenhouse gas carbon dioxide belched out of the Earth too, turning the climate blazing hot.

A few years after the eruptions stopped, Earth was left barren and nearly lifeless. Over 90 percent of all species were gone—both on land and in the sea. Scientists call it the End-Permian Extinction. It is the worst mass extinction the Earth has ever seen.

SUPERVOLCANOES

Supervolcanoes have the power to change global climate. These massive volcanoes form where superhot magma rises from the mantle and builds up beneath Earth's crust. Eventually the pressure becomes too great, and the supervolcano erupts, spewing lava across the land, and dust and toxic gases into the atmosphere. The damage caused can be thousands of times as serious as a regular volcanic eruption. Climate change and choking ash can cause species to go extinct across the globe.

Scientists are monitoring a supervolcano sleeping beneath Yellowstone National Park in Wyoming.

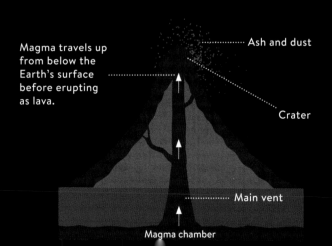

Magma travels up from below the Earth's surface before erupting as lava.

Ash and dust

Crater

Main vent

Magma chamber

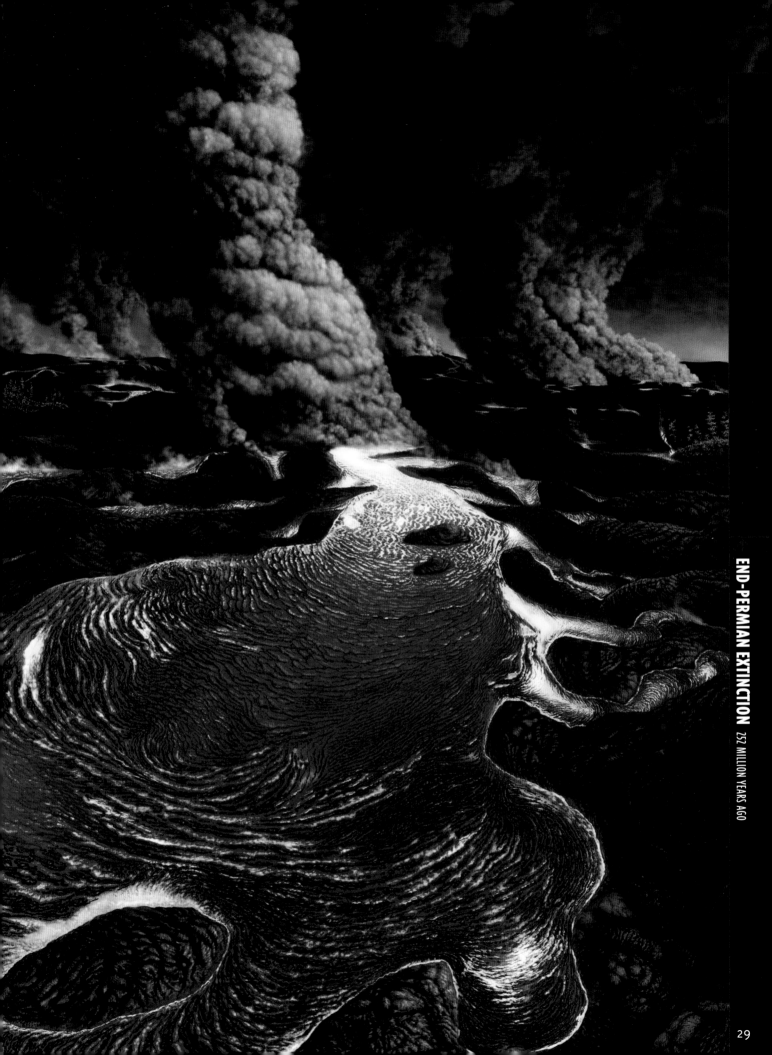

END-PERMIAN EXTINCTION *252 MILLION YEARS AGO*

PERMIAN

299–252 MILLION YEARS AGO

As the Permian Period began, two huge land masses were slowly colliding to form the supercontinent Pangea. Over the course of only a few million years, many places became much warmer and dryer. A small new group of animals that had developed the ability to lay shelled eggs found success in this changing environment. A tough, or hard-shelled, egg is like a little portable pond that can be laid almost anywhere.

The largest-known insects lived during this period. Close relatives of dragonflies, the biggest griffinflies had wingspans of up to 25 inches (64 cm) across.

Among these egg-layers were the first mammal-relatives. But these animals didn't seem much like mammals today. They included low-slung, scaly hunters with sails on their back, such as *Dimetrodon*. The first true reptiles, which also laid shelled eggs, lived at this time too. In almost every ecosystem, other animals such as the amphibians were now facing some stiff competition. Amphibians are a group of animals that are born in water, and most need to stay close by it during their adult lives too.

Land ecosystems in the Permian were filled with a great variety of animals. But by today's standards, Permian ecosystems were weird. The Early Permian was a predator-eat-predator world. There were plenty of plants, but there were very few big plant-eaters! It was mainly insects that took advantage of the nutritious ferns, cycads, conifers, and horsetails that covered the land. Most large animals—amphibians, reptiles, and our early-mammal-relatives—simply refused to eat their vegetables. It wasn't until the Late Permian, 260 million years ago, that many types of big plant-eaters appeared and modern ecosystems developed.

Today in nearly every ecosystem, plant-eaters far outnumber meat-eaters. A few predators can be found at the top of the food web, with many different types and great numbers of plant-eaters for them to feed on. At the base of the web, there are lots and lots of plants.

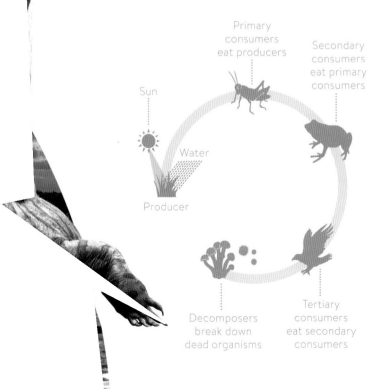

Primary consumers eat producers

Secondary consumers eat primary consumers

Sun

Water

Producer

Decomposers break down dead organisms

Tertiary consumers eat secondary consumers

FOOD CHAINS AND FOOD WEBS

A single ecosystem can contain a huge variety of living things. Plants use the Sun's energy to produce their own food from water, carbon dioxide from the air, and minerals from the soil. Many animals feed on the plants, and some feed on each other. Each system of connections in an ecosystem is called a food chain.

Put all the food chains in an ecosystem together, and you have a food web. Food webs show how all the species in an ecosystem are connected to, and depend upon, each other. Remove a single species from the food web and the whole ecosystem can be affected.

CARBONIFEROUS

359–299 MILLION YEARS AGO

In the Carboniferous Period, you might find it difficult to spot the animals hidden among the lush ferns and giant trees. Forests of woody club mosses, called lycopsids, grew as straight as telephone poles, towering over the swamps. Their scale tree relatives showed off their beautifully patterned branches and stems. Tree-sized ferns grew taller than ten-story buildings. Horsetails and vine-like ferns carpeted the soggy understory.

Plant-eating arthropods of many kinds enjoyed this food paradise. Giant dragonflies nibbled the high, leafy fronds, cockroaches tunneled into the trunks, and millipedes the size of coffee tables fed on the rotting wood below.

Amphibians ruled the Carboniferous swamps, but a strange new type of creature appeared around this time as well. They looked like small lizards. They had dry, scaly skin too. These were the world's first reptiles.

In the Carboniferous, most of Earth's continents were grouped together near the South Pole. Winters were snowy, and not all of the snow melted during the summers. Over time, ice sheets spread out across millions of square miles. Earth was in an ice age—similar to the Ice Age we are in today.

The earliest reptiles, such as *Hylonomus*, lived during the Carboniferous Period.

Carboniferous swamp

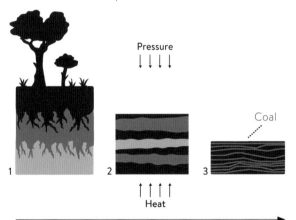

Pressure

↓ ↓ ↓ ↓

Coal

1   2   3

↑ ↑ ↑ ↑

Heat

Time →

COAL

The coal we burn today to generate electricity formed over 300 million years ago in the Carboniferous Period (1). As the giant trees and other plants died and fell into the swamps, they turned into a dark, crumbly substance called peat. Over millions of years, many layers of peat were buried deeper and deeper underground. Pressure from above and heat from deep inside the Earth (2) transformed the peat into the hard black rock we call coal (3).

The seas of the Carboniferous seem to have been a haven for some of the world's weirdest sharks. With unusual teeth and fins, they were the top marine predators of the time.

DEVONIAN

At start of the Devonian Period you wouldn't find a single animal with four legs! The only plants around you would be small and found close to water. But a big change was about to happen.

During this period, the first trees with strong, woody stems appeared. Forests began to take root in areas that had once been barren land. Soon the whole world was transformed. The forests provided food and shelter for a variety of new animals.

In the oceans, lakes, and streams, predatory fish with tough armor and strong jaws were flourishing. A few types of animals began to venture out of the water, leaving their tracks in the mud. Breathing air on land wasn't easy, but any animal able to live out of the water, even for part of its life, could avoid being eaten by these fierce fish.

The first insects and spiders arrived on the scene during this time. These animals are part of the arthropod group, which includes insects, spiders, crabs, and many others. Today they are the most numerous animal group on Earth.

The first four-legged animals crawled ashore too. Salamander-like *Ichthyostega* lived mainly in lakes and streams, but it could walk out on land to hunt. It is one of the earliest relatives of all amphibians. Under the protective shade of the spreading forests, and with plenty of insects and spiders to eat, amphibians soon conquered the land.

Rhyniella was a springtail (a close relative of insects) and was one of the earliest arthropods on land.

FINS TO FEET

Four-legged animals first crawled ashore around 395 million years ago. All of them descended from a type of fish that had four sturdy, lobe-shaped fins. These fish could use their fins to "walk" through shallow water and mud. Some of them even had lungs for breathing air, in addition to the gills that let them breathe in water. Over time, the descendants of these fish developed sturdier, more flexible limbs and began spending most of their adult lives out of water.

Insects

Other animals

Insects alone make up more than half of all animal species on Earth.

SILURIAN

443–419 MILLION YEARS AGO

Temperatures were slowly rising on Earth as the Silurian Period began. New life-forms took hold in the warmer environments. Among the most important of the new arrivals were the first fish with jaws. Jaws allowed sophisticated predators, such as the spiny shark *Nerepisacanthus*, to take over the oceans.

Take a bite of your sandwich and pause for a moment to appreciate the first jawed fish of the Silurian. Over the millions of years since then, many types of jawed animals have lived on Earth. And all of them—from *T. rex* to you—inherited their chompers from these early fish.

Alongside the jawed fish were weird scorpion-like arthropods called eurypterids. These marine predators used their powerful pincers to grab and pull apart prey. Some eurypterids grew to incredible sizes, such as *Carcinosoma*, which could reach nearly 8 feet (2.5 m) in length!

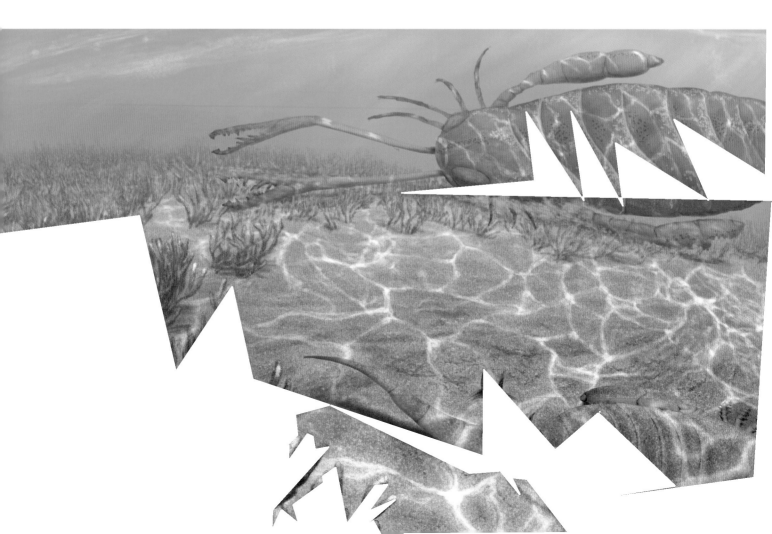

SURVIVING ON LAND

During the Silurian Period, land plants such as *Cooksonia* developed a new kind of plumbing system. Little tubes inside their stems helped them bring water up from their roots to their branches and leaves. This meant they could grow up and away from the water, while still staying hydrated.

These vascular plants could only grow a few inches high, but they towered over the green algae and little mosses that had been the only plants on land for millions of years. Today, vascular plants are the tallest life-forms on Earth. Redwood trees in California can reach heights over 350 feet (105 m).

The thick protective armor around the head of many Silurian fish, such as *Psarolepis*, was formed of bony plates.

Early plants such as *Cooksonia* had simple branches without leaves.

Vascular plants contain tubes for transporting water and minerals up from the soil and through the plant.

ORDOVICIAN

485–443 MILLION YEARS AGO

If you traveled back 485 million years to the Ordovician Period, you'd see nothing but a sun-baked, barren landscape, with patches of slimy green algae clinging to the rocks. All the action was in the sea!

If you put on your snorkeling gear, you could swim over the sunlit, sandy bottom. Here you'd see green algae, lacy-looking bryozoans, and some of the world's first corals. You might see swarms of conodonts—weird eel-shaped creatures with buggy eyes and complicated teeth. Snails, clams, nautiloids, trilobites, and a whole array of other invertebrates made their homes here as well.

In these sunlit waters, you would also come face to face with some of the world's first fish. Sucking up bits of food from the ocean bottom, *Astrapsis* may have looked like an oversized tadpole, but don't let its goofy look fool you. It was one of the first ancestors of the group of animals with backbones—the vertebrates. This large group of animals includes all fish, amphibians, reptiles, birds, and mammals (including us!)

Corals

The Great Barrier Reef covers an area of around 133,000 square miles (344,400 square km). That's about the same size as the whole of Japan!

CORAL REEFS

Corals began to spread across the globe in the Ordovician Period. They might look like plants, but corals are simple animals. Inside the cells of many corals are algae, which give them their vibrant colors. The corals partially rely on these algae, which use energy from sunlight to make their food.

Over time, corals form reefs along the seabed. Like underwater forests, coral reef ecosystems are home to a huge number of other species. Unfortunately, many reefs are under threat today because of pollution and warming seas.

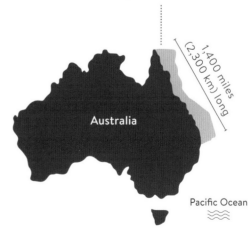

1,400 miles (2,300 km) long

Australia

Pacific Ocean

CAMBRIAN

Worm-like *Pikaia* hid a remarkable secret. A flexible rod ran down the whole length of its body, giving it strength. This could make *Pikaia* the ancestor of the vertebrates—the animal group that includes fish, amphibians, reptiles, birds, and mammals.

In the oceans around 540 million years ago, complex animals with many different forms began to spread out across the seafloor. So many new animal types appeared so quickly that paleontologists call it the Cambrian Explosion.

Cambrian animals sported an extraordinary array of hard parts: shells, spines, plates, and skeletons. And that was a very good thing because the Cambrian was the period when animals first began eating other animals. Over time, predators became faster swimmers, with stronger senses for detecting prey, including better vision and eyes. They developed fancy new features that helped them grab, drill, or nip their prey. In turn, their prey developed hard shells, prickly spikes, and armor plates to defend themselves.

One group that is worth a closer look were trilobites. But don't be surprised to find the trilobites looking back at you! Trilobites were early arthropods, with segmented shells and jointed legs. There were so many kinds of trilobites in the Cambrian, it's sometimes called the Age of Trilobites.

Trilobites came in many forms. Some were plain, and some were covered with ornate spikes and spines. Most were small, but some could grow to be over 2 feet (0.6 m) long. The last trilobites died out during the End-Permian Extinction. That means their group survived for around 250 million years.

| Sponge | Vertebrate | Annelid worm | Mollusk | Arthropod |

Cambrian body plans

The basic body plans of most of today's animal groups developed in the Cambrian Period.

CAMBRIAN EXPLOSION

The Cambrian ocean may look like an alien, watery world, but this is where most of the major animal groups we know today appeared. It is here that the long, amazing story of life began to take some incredible turns.

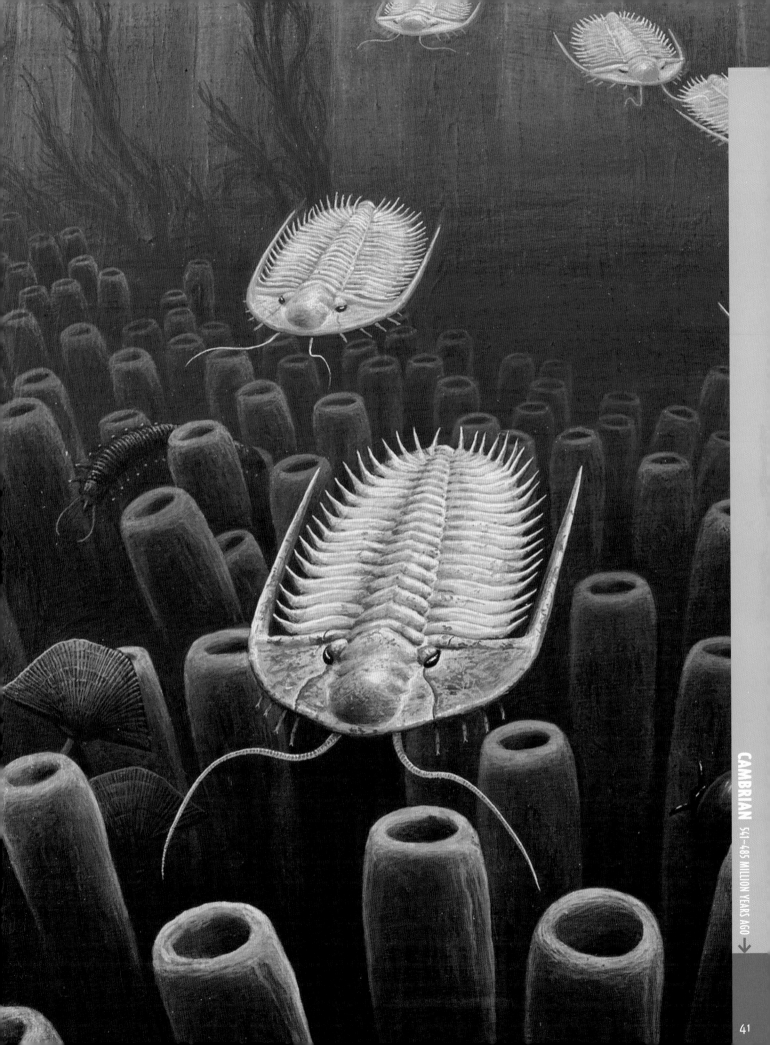

EDIACARAN AND BEFORE

4.6 BILLION–541 MILLION YEARS AGO

This section represents all of the time we've covered so far—a period of around 541 million years.

Mysterious soft-bodied animals first appeared in the ocean during the Ediacaran Period, which began 625 million years ago. Most of these creatures are poorly understood, and their connection to life today isn't known for certain.

But Earth's first life-forms appeared long before this. They were so tiny that you'd need to use a microscope just to see them. These simple life-forms appeared around 3.5 billion years ago. That's about 7 times as long ago as the stretch of time we've covered so far. Back then, the Earth was swelteringly hot, and there was very little oxygen in the air. So, if you were planning to visit, you'd need to wear a space suit with a life-support system.

Life today comes in a huge variety of forms. But most of these forms only evolved in the last 540 million years. Take a look at the new timeline on the right—this timeline shows the full story of life on Earth.

How much has life on Earth changed in this time? We may seldom think about them, because we can't see them, but most of the living things on Earth right now are tiny, single-celled bacteria and archaea—much like the most ancient, simple life-forms. We and all the other animals, plants, and fungi make up only a small (and relatively recent!) part of the tree of life.

AGE OF THE EARTH

The story of life may be a long one, but the Earth's own story goes back even further. Scientists think the Earth is around 4.6 billion years old, based on the age of the oldest known rocks and minerals.

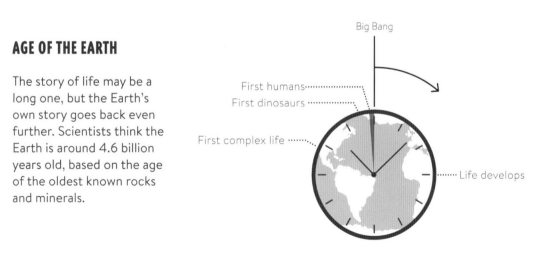

If the whole story of the Earth were shown on a 12-hour clock, all of human history would only take up the last 3 minutes.

GLOSSARY

AMPHIBIANS
Vertebrate animals that usually have smooth, moist skin and lay their eggs in water. Adults mostly live on land and breathe air. Frogs and salamanders are examples of amphibians.

ANGIOSPERM
A type of plant with flowers that produce seeds. Most leafy trees, shrubs, grasses, and garden flowers are angiosperms.

ANTHROPOCENE
The time period we live in today. During this period human activities, such as the burning of fossil fuels, have begun to cause rapid changes in the Earth's systems.

ARCHOSAUR
A group of egg-laying **vertebrates**. Archosaur skulls have two openings behind each eye. The group includes all crocodilians, pterosaurs, dinosaurs, and birds.

ARTHROPOD
Invertebrate animals with a stiff outer-covering, segmented body, and jointed legs. Insects, spiders, millipedes, and crustaceans are some examples.

ASTEROID
One of millions of small, planet-like bodies in the solar system. Most orbit the Sun in the asteroid belt. Rarely, one may be knocked from its orbit and approach the Earth.

BACTERIA
Microscopic, single-celled living things. Bacteria are abundant everywhere on Earth.

CARBON DIOXIDE
One of the main **greenhouse gases** in Earth's atmosphere. Carbon dioxide is colorless and odorless. It is produced when carbon combines with oxygen during burning or respiration.

CONIFER
A type of tree that bears seeds in cones. Usually conifers have evergreen, needle-shaped leaves. Pine trees and fir trees are examples of conifers.

CORALS
Small **invertebrate** sea animals that have hard skeletons. Individual corals, called polyps, form large colonies. Together, the hard parts of many corals can form a reef.

EXTINCTION
When a species dies out completely and not one individual remains alive.

FUNGI
Neither plants nor animals, fungi are living things that reproduce by spores. Most feed on dead or decaying matter. Mushrooms and molds are two examples of fungi.

GLACIER
A huge, thick sheet of ice that moves very slowly across the land. Glaciers form when more snow falls than melts each summer.

GREENHOUSE GASES
Any gas that traps the Sun's heat in the atmosphere. **Carbon dioxide**, water vapor, methane, and nitrous oxide are the main examples.

INVERTEBRATE
Any animal without a backbone. Insects, crustaceans, and mollusks (such as clams and snails) are examples of invertebrates.

MAMMALS
Vertebrate animals that have fur, or at least some hair, on their bodies. Mammals feed their babies milk from the mother's body. Most types give birth to live young.

PLANKTON
Tiny living things that float or drift in vast numbers in the world's oceans. Plankton form the base of the food chain in ocean ecosystems.

REPTILES
Air-breathing **vertebrate** animals that have dry, scaly skin and lay tough-shelled eggs on land. Crocodilians, snakes, and lizards are examples of reptiles.

SUPERCONTINENT
A huge land mass made up of several continent-sized plates stuck together. Supercontinents slowly form and break apart due to the motions of plate tectonics.

VERTEBRATE
Any animal that has a backbone. Fish, **amphibians**, **reptiles**, birds, and **mammals** are vertebrates.

INDEX

PAGES 8-9

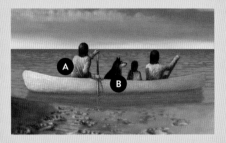

A - Human
B - Dog

PAGE 10

A - *Glyptotherium*
B - *Eremotherium*

PAGES 12-13

A - *Gompotherium*
B - Rat snake
C - Passerine bird
D - Grasshopper
E - *Ceratogaulus*

PAGE 13

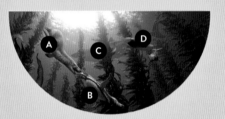

A - *Acrophoca*
B - Banded penguin
C - *Eurhinodelphis*
D - Megalodon shark

PAGE 15

A - *Presbyornis*

PAGE 19

A - *Gorgosaurus*
B - *Spinops*

PAGE 20

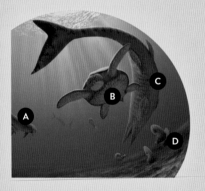

A - *Icthyodectes*
B - *Protostega*
C - *Tylosaurus*
D - *Placenticeras*

PAGE 22

A - *Apatosaurus*
B - *Harpactognathus*

PAGES 24-25

A - *Smilosuchus*
B - *Chindesaurus*
C - *Desmatosuchus*